This Book
Belongs to

Brief History of Airplanes

The aspiration to fly dates back to the earliest days of humanity. Nonetheless, the airplane concept has a more recent history, spanning just two centuries. Preceding this period, individuals sought to traverse the skies by emulating birds, crafting wings to attach to their arms or constructing machines with flapping wings, known as ornithopters. At first glance, this approach appeared promising, given the abundance of airborne birds that served as evidence of the concept's viability. The challenge in achieving flight lies in the fact that the concept, effective on the scale of birds, struggles when applied to the larger scale required for lifting both humans and machines. This led to the exploration of alternative flight methods. Beginning in 1783, a few aeronauts attempted uncontrolled flights using lighter-than-air balloons filled with hot air or hydrogen gas. However, this approach proved impractical due to the lack of reliable navigation unless the wind happened to blow in the desired direction.

In the early 19th century, Sir George Cayley, an English baronet from Yorkshire, conceptualized the fundamental idea of the airplane—a flying machine featuring fixed wings, a propulsion system, and movable control surfaces. Cayley's innovation materialized in the form of the first true airplane, a basic kite with a movable tail. Despite its simplicity, this humble glider demonstrated the viability of his concept. From this initial achievement, evolved the remarkable machines that have propelled humanity to the edge of space, achieving speeds faster than sound.

Richard Branson next to a replica of Sir George Cayley's glider

In 1874, Felix du Temple undertook the inaugural powered flight attempt by launching off a ramp in a steam-driven monoplane. Concurrently, scientists like Francis Wenham and Horatio Phillips examined cambered wing designs in wind tunnels and on rotating arms. It wasn't until 1894 that Sir Hiram Maxim achieved a successful takeoff (albeit an uncontrollable flight) in a biplane "test rig." Meanwhile, Otto Lilienthal achieved the first controlled flights by skillfully adjusting his body weight to steer a small glider.

Motivated by Lilienthal's achievements, Wilbur and Orville Wright began experimenting with aerodynamic surfaces to master airplane control. Their diligent efforts culminated in the historic accomplishment of the first controlled, sustained, and powered flights on December 17, 1903, in Kitty Hawk, North Carolina.

Following their initial powered flights in 1903, the Wright Brothers embark on transforming their experimental aircraft into a marketable product. By 1905, they achieve what they deem a "practical flying machine." Other aviation enthusiasts learn of their progress and begin building upon their success. By 1906, aspiring pilots are attempting tentative flights in aircraft that lack control. By 1909, having witnessed the Wrights' demonstrations, they recognize the brilliance and necessity of three-axis aerodynamic control. The performance of their aircraft rapidly catches up to and surpasses Wright Flyers.

A replica of the Wright Brothers 1905 Wright Flyer III flying

In 1911, the Vin Fiz, an aircraft designed by the Wright Brothers, became the first airplane to traverse the United States. The journey, spanning 84 days with 70 stops, resulted in numerous crash landings, leaving little of its original construction intact by the time it reached California. Named after a grape soda produced by the Armour Packing Company, the Vin Fiz made a historic cross-country flight.

Following the Wright Brothers, inventors continued enhancing aircraft technology, eventually leading to the creation of jets, utilized by both military and commercial airlines. A jet, powered by jet engines, operates at significantly higher speeds and altitudes compared to propeller-driven aircraft, with some reaching heights of 10,000 to 15,000 meters (approximately 33,000 to 49,000 feet). The credit for the development of the jet engine in the late 1930s goes to engineers Frank Whittle from the United Kingdom and Hans von Ohain from Germany.

Since then, certain companies have pioneered the development of electric aircraft, utilizing electric motors instead of internal combustion engines. The electricity powering these aircraft is sourced from alternative fuel options such as fuel cells, solar cells, ultracapacitors, power beaming, and batteries. Despite being in its early stages, some production models of electric aircraft are already available in the market.

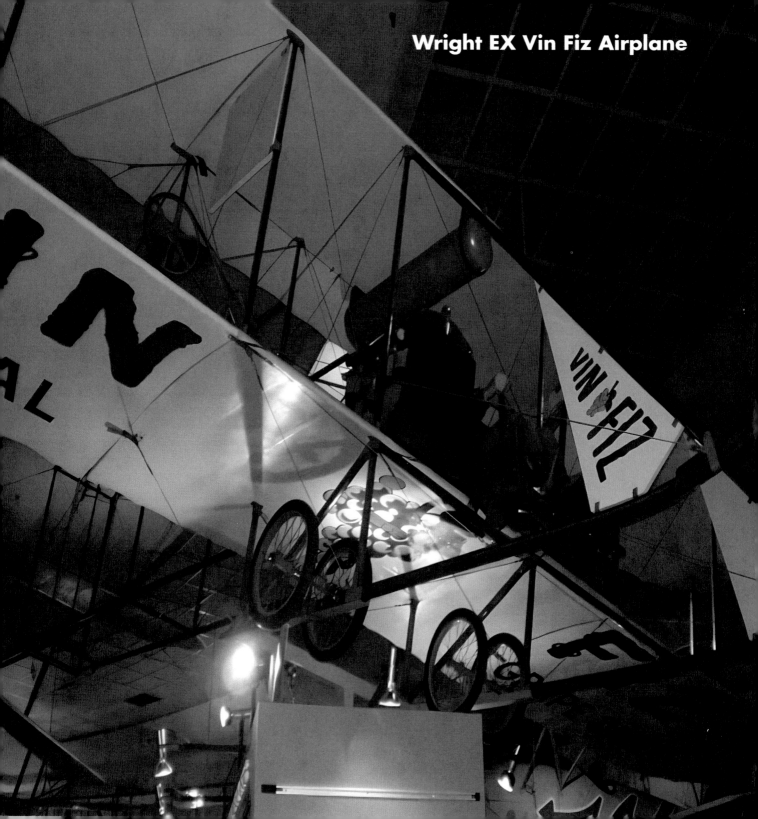

Another realm of exploration involves rocket-powered aircraft. These airplanes employ engines that utilize rocket propellant for propulsion, enabling them to attain higher speeds and faster acceleration. For instance, during World War II, the Germans deployed the Me 163 Komet as an early rocket-powered aircraft. The Bell X-1 rocket plane made history in 1947 by becoming the first aircraft to break the sound barrier.

Presently, the North American X-15 holds the world record for the highest speed ever recorded by a manned, powered aircraft. Some pioneering companies have also delved into experimenting with rocket-powered propulsion, exemplified by projects like SpaceShipOne, designed by American aerospace engineer Burt Rutan, and Virgin Galactic's SpaceShipTwo.

Virgin Galactic's SpaceShipTwo

Airplanes That Changed the World

The first airplane to cross the English Channel.

Blériot XI

Motivated by the Wright Brothers' innovative use of wing warping in flying, aviation trailblazer Louis Blériot adapted his unique monoplane with the goal of becoming the first individual to cross the English Channel in a heavier-than-air aircraft. His successful feat triggered a cultural realization that aviation wasn't merely a pastime for affluent individuals but could serve as a valuable tool to connect the world. The demand for Blériot's design surged, and many contemporaneous aviation pioneers embraced variations of his aircraft. Among them was Clyde Cessna, the founder of the Cessna Aircraft Corporation, a company that holds the record for selling more single-engine aircraft than any other.

Supermarine Spitfire

The Spitfire, the only British fighter continuously produced throughout World War II, played a crucial role in the Battle of Britain, known for its distinctive elliptical wings and versatile functions, serving as an interceptor, photo reconnaissance, fighter-bomber, and trainer. Initially powered by a Rolls-Royce Merlin engine, it later adapted to the powerful Griffon engine.

The only aircraft built throughout the World War II.

Spitfire flying over East Sussex at the Eastbourne Air Show, 14th August 2015, England, UK

Boeing 787

the Boeing Dreamliner is the company's first airliner primarily constructed from composite materials, featuring a unique fuselage assembly, innovative wing design, and a fly-by-wire flight system. Despite development challenges, the Dreamliner sets new standards for fuel efficiency, quietness, and lightweight design in the aviationindustry.

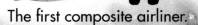

The first composite airliner.

Lockheed SR-71 Blackbird

The Lockheed SR-71 Blackbird, a marvel of Cold War-era engineering, is renowned for its unparalleled speed and altitude capabilities. Developed by Lockheed's Skunk Works division in the 1960s, the reconnaissance aircraft could soar at speeds exceeding Mach 3 and operate at altitudes surpassing 85,000 feet. Its sleek, titanium construction and strategic design made it a formidable asset for high-stakes intelligence-gathering missions. Retired in 1998, the SR-71 remains an enduring symbol of aerospace innovation, leaving an indelible mark on aviation history.

Cirrus SR22

In 2001, the SR22 made a significant impact on the general aviation community and has maintained its position as the top-selling single-engine, four-seat aircraft for over a decade. Featuring composite construction and equipped with an airframe ballistic parachute, this streamlined Cirrus instilled confidence in novice pilots, empowering them to handle a high-performance aircraft. Ryan Campbell, in 2013, utilized the SR22 when he achieved the distinction of being the youngest pilot to complete a solo circumnavigation of the globe. Notably, the parachute system is attributed to saving over 100 lives.

Learjet 23

In 1960, Bill Lear relocated from California to Switzerland to establish the Swiss American Aviation Corporation, aiming to revamp the FFA P-16 ground attack fighter prototype. Despite the setback of the SAAC-23 ExecutJet cancellation by Switzerland, Lear persisted. Recognizing a burgeoning market for executive business travel, he returned to the U.S. and developed the Learjet 23, ushering in a new era of swift and efficient business aircraft. Transitioning under a new name and country, Learjet manufactured 104 aircraft at its Kansas facility within just two years, concluding in 1966. Capable of carrying eight passengers at 560 mph, it became the inaugural mass-produced business jet, solidifying the term "Learjet" as synonymous with the concept of a business jet.

Cirrus SR22

Lockheed C-130

Renowned for its unparalleled flexibility, the C-130 has earned a reputation as the most adaptable and versatile workhorse within the armed forces. Initially conceived as a troop and cargo transport for operation on unimproved runways, this aircraft has evolved into a multi-role platform, serving as a gunship, supporting 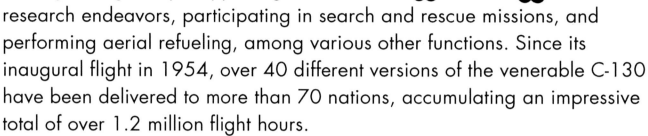 research endeavors, participating in search and rescue missions, and performing aerial refueling, among various other functions. Since its inaugural flight in 1954, over 40 different versions of the venerable C-130 have been delivered to more than 70 nations, accumulating an impressive total of over 1.2 million flight hours.

Douglas DC-3

The DC-3, introduced in 1936, significantly transformed American air travel, possibly ranking as the aircraft with the most substantial impact on transportation habits. Before its arrival, cross-country flights from Los Angeles to New York were laborious, involving up to 15 stops, multiple airline changes, and the use of two or three different airplanes. The DC-3 revolutionized this by enabling a single aircraft, accommodating 20 passengers, to cross the country in about 15 hours with only three fueling stops. Douglas's innovative features, including supercharged engines, cantilevered metal wings, and retractable landing gear.

Douglas DC3 Dakota restored and owned and opperated from Norway.

Cessna 172

The Cessna 172 Skyhawk holds the record for the highest number of sales among all aircraft. Introduced in 1956, this four-seat, single-engine, high-wing personal aircraft has surpassed 43,000 units sold and continues to be in production today. Known for its reliability, affordability, and stability, the Skyhawk has become a fundamental choice for flight training schools globally. Its enduring performance and widespread use make it an ideal mode of transportation for private pilots worldwide. The success of the Skyhawk played a pivotal role in establishing the Cessna Aircraft Company's dominance in the light aircraft market.

Boeing B-29 Superfortress

The B-29 is renowned for delivering the decisive blows to Japan in WWII through the deployment of atomic bombs on Hiroshima and Nagasaki. While this historic event alone merits the Superfortress a significant place among pivotal aircraft, it's crucial to acknowledge the aircraft's remarkable technological innovations ahead of its time. Notably, it featured an ingenious remote firing system for turret machine guns, dual-wheeled tricycle landing gear, and a pressurized cabin. In subsequent years, with the addition of new engines and its redesignation as the B-50, this aircraft achieved another milestone by becoming the first to circumnavigate the globe nonstop.

The only flying WWII Boeing B-29 Superfortress called FIFI

Gulfstream G500

The private business jet, introduced with the G600 in 2014, features advanced fly-by-wire technology originally used in military aircraft. The active side-stick provides visual and tactile feedback for both the pilot and copilot, allowing them to monitor each other's inputs and autopilot controls. The Honeywell Symmetry flight deck displays flight instruments through 10 touchscreen controllers, offering comprehensive access to system controls, flight management, communication tools, checklists, and real-time weather and flight information.

Boeing 747

The original jumbo jet, the Boeing 747, held the passenger capacity record for 37 years, recognized by the distinctive upper deck hump reserved for first-class passengers. It was more than twice the size of any existing airliner at the time, with engineers manually sketching 75,000 technical drawings and constructing a full-scale plywood mockup to ensure precision. Boeing even erected the world's largest building to manufacture this colossal aircraft. Although initially anticipated to be a transitional solution until the development of a supersonic transport, the 747's success exceeded expectations, with over 1,500 units sold to date and numerous additional orders, making it an enduring masterpiece of industrial design that temporarily slowed advancements in passenger aviation.

Boeing 747-422 N104UA in flight over the sea

Bell X-1

The X-1 is a famous supersonic research aircraft, breaking the sound barrier in 1947 and marking the first in the series of X-planes. These experimental aircraft, including the X-1, were instrumental in testing advanced systems and aerodynamics, contributing valuable lessons that played a role in propelling the United States into space. The supersonic flight data collected from X-1 tests also proved crucial for the design of future U.S. fighter jets.

Spirit of St. Louis

Ryan NYP, known as the "Spirit of St. Louis," was the aircraft that carried Charles Lindbergh on his historic non-stop flight across the Atlantic in 1927. Lindbergh collaborated with the Ryan Aircraft Company to design this single-engine aircraft, and its success had an immediate and transformative impact on aviation. The flight boosted Lindbergh to fame and significantly increased interest in aviation, leading to a surge in pilot license applications, a rise in licensed aircraft, and a substantial growth in airline passengers in the years that followed.

Dassault Falcon 7X

The French-built business jet, incorporating technology from Dassault's Mirage military fighter, boasts innovative design processes, including the pioneering use of Computer Aided Three-Dimensional Interactive Application (CATIA) software.

CATIA, initially developed by Dassault for jet fighters, was later utilized by Boeing for the design of the 777 and 787.

Dassault Falcon 7X

The F-16, renowned as one of the most important planes ever built, boasts exceptional speed, altitude capabilities, and maneuverability. Its frameless bubble canopy offers unprecedented visibility, and a reclined seating position mitigates the effects of g-forces on the pilot. The F-16 was the first fighter designed to be aerodynamically unstable, enhancing maneuverability through a computer-augmented fly-by-wire system. With over 4,500 units produced since 1976, it is a staple in the military fleets of over 25 nations.

Dassault Falcon 7X

RV-3

Richard VanGrunsven's decision to leave his job and construct an airplane in his garage marked the

inception of the most successful aircraft kit-building company in history. Beginning with a modified Sitts Playboy named RV-1, he pursued aerobatic excellence, leading to the creation of the RV-3—a single-seat taildragger capable of reaching 200 mph with just 150 horsepower. Over four decades, VanGrunsven expanded his line of successful kit aircraft, with more than 8,500 DIYers completing and flying their RVs. The company's annual production now surpasses that of all commercial general aviation companies combined, highlighting the enduring success of VanGrunsven's innovative designs.

Scaled Composites Voyager

Conceived from a napkin sketch by Burt Rutan, this unique high-endurance aircraft, piloted by Dick Rutan and Jeana Yeager, achieved the historic feat of circumnavigating the globe without stopping or refueling. Featuring one forward- and one rear-facing propeller attached to separate engines, the aircraft maintained an average altitude of 11,000 feet and a speed of 116 mph during its nine-day non-stop journey from Edwards Air Force Base in California.

Amazing Facts About Airplanes

1 The world's smallest jet is the BD-5 Micro. Its wingspan is 14–21 feet and weighs just 358 pounds.

2 One windshield or window frame of a Boeing 747-400's cockpit costs as much as a BMW.

3 The global aviation community has designated English as the universal language for flight. It is mandatory for flight controllers and commercial pilots engaged in international flights to communicate in English.

4 The emergency oxygen masks on an airplane provide a supply of oxygen that typically lasts for approximately 15 minutes.

5 The average price of building an airplane ranges from $90 to $115M, depending on its size and capability.

6 With a wingspan of 288 feet (87 m), a weight of 710 tons, and six engines, the Antonov An-225 Mriya was the largest and heaviest operational airplane until Russia destroyed it in 2022.

7 The plane's famous "black box" is not black but orange because it'd be more visible in case of an accident.

8 Less than 10 people witnessed the first powered flight by the Wright Brothers on December 17, 1903. The distance flown by the Wright Brothers that day (about 120 ft) was less than the wingspan of today's Boeing 747- which is about 210 feet.

9 The probability of dying in a plane crash is one in 11M, while the possibility of dying in a car crash is one in 5K. That means your chances of dying in a car accident are 2.2K times higher than in a plane crash.

Antonov An-225 Mriya aircraft takes off.

10 The Airbus A380 is the largest passenger plane that can carry up to 850 people.

11 There are an average of 10,000 planes in the sky at any one time carrying roughly 1 million passengers.

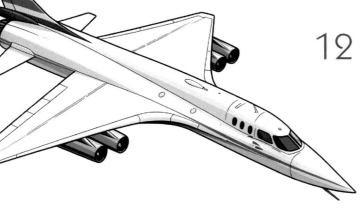

12 In 1996, the Concorde set the record flying time from New York to London-making the journey in only 2 hours, 52 minutes, and 59 seconds and traveling at speeds of up to 1,354 mph. The Concorde would later be retired in 2003.

13 The altitude at which commercial aircraft usually fly is between 33,000 and 42,000 feet (10 and 12.8 km). It's called cruising altitude.

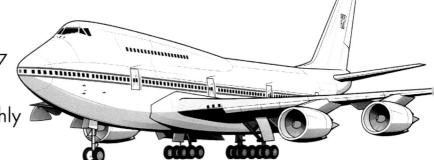

14 The average Boeing 747 has around 150–175 miles of wiringand roughly 6 million parts inside it.

15 There have been more astronauts than pilots who have flown the Concorde.

The Concorde

16 The world's fastest airplane is the Lockheed SR-71 Blackbird, flying at 2,193 miles per hour. It has held the record for nearly 40 years.

17 Commercial airport runways are typically 2 to 4 feet thick with layers of asphalt. Taxiways are usually thinner, with around 18 inches of concrete.

18 The probability of dying in a plane crash is one in 11M, while the possibility of dying in a car crash is one in 5K. That means your chances of dying in a car accident are 2.2K times higher than in a plane crash.

19 The world's busiest airport is the Hartsfield-Jackson Atlanta International Airport, at over 96 million passengers a year. Beijing Capital International Airport is in second place, with more than 86 million passengers a year. However, Chicago's O'Hare is the busiest in the world in terms of take offs and landings.

Passenger airplane on the airfield docked with a passenger boarding bridge

20 The atmosphere in an airplane cabin dries out a person's nose, and the changing air pressure numbs about 1/3 of a person's taste buds. This is one reason for airlines adding lots of spices and salt to their foods. Additionally, tomato juice tastes less acidic in the air.

21 According to Popular Mechanics, sitting in the tail of an airplane improves chances of accident survival by 40%.

22 Mercury is not allowed on a flight. Even a small amount of mercury can seriously damage aluminum, which is what most planes are made from. Airplanes that are exposed to mercury are usually quarantined.

23 A pilot must have 20/20 vision, with or without corrective lenses, to become a civilian airline pilot.

24 The main components of airplanes are titanium, steel, and aluminum.

25 There are an average of 10,000 planes in the sky at any one time carrying roughly 1 million passengers.

26 In 1986, a plane called Voyager flew all the way around the world without landing or refueling.

27 Plane exhaust kills more people than plane crashes. Approximately, 10,000 people are killed annually from toxic pollutants from airplanes.

28 One the most deadly airplane accidents actually happened on the ground. In 1977, two fully loaded planes carrying a total of over 600 passengers collided head-on in the middle of the runway in what is now known as the Tenerife Accident, named after Tenerife Island where the accident occurred. Over 500 people died.

29 The largest private jet belongs to Joseph Lau and is valued at $367M. It has an interior of 1,460 square feet (135 sq m) and a spiral staircase connecting the two levels.

30 Antarctica has 20 airports, but they all have limited and non-public access.

31 The world's shortest commercial flight lasts only 80 seconds and travels only 16.77 miles (26.9 km)—the distance between the islands of Papa Westray and Westray in Scotland.

32 Commercial airplanes are struck by lightning an average of two times yearly. Even so, aircraft are prepared to withstand a discharge of that power and avoid significant damage.

Thank You and we hope you enjoyed our Book.

Please leave us your review.

It will take you only few minutes and it means a lot to us.

Thank You

For more interesting picture books please visit us on Amazon at Medina Creative.

Made in the USA
Monee, IL
03 November 2024

69254502R00026